THIS JOURNAL BELONGS TO:

Visit us at www.seashellsandstorytime.com
or connect with us on Facebook at
Facebook.com/seashellsandstorytime.

We love hearing from you!

First Printing: 2019

ISBN 9781086819960

Seashells and Storytime
Freeport, Maine
Stacey@seashellsandstorytime.com
www.seashellsandstorytime.com

Today's Date: _____

What are you grateful for today?

_____

_____

_____

_____

Today's highlights:

_____

_____

_____

_____

Today's challenges:

_____

_____

_____

_____

What are your goals for this year?

_____

_____

_____

_____

_____

Today's Date: _____

What are you grateful for today?

_____

_____

_____

_____

Today's highlights:

_____

_____

_____

_____

Today's challenges:

_____

_____

_____

_____

If you could have one superpower, what would it be?

_____

_____

_____

_____

Today's Date: _____

What are you grateful for today?

_____

_____

_____

_____

Today's highlights:

_____

_____

_____

_____

Today's challenges:

_____

_____

_____

_____

What are your 3 best qualities?

_____

_____

_____

_____

_____

Today's Date: _____

What are you grateful for today?

_____

_____

_____

_____

Today's highlights:

_____

_____

_____

_____

Today's challenges:

_____

_____

_____

_____

Where would you live if you could pick anywhere in the world?

_____

_____

_____

_____

_____

Today's Date: _____

What are you grateful for today?

_____

_____

_____

_____

Today's highlights:

_____

_____

_____

_____

Today's challenges:

_____

_____

_____

_____

If you could have dinner with 3 people, who would you pick?

_____

_____

_____

_____

Today's Date: _____

What are you grateful for today?

_____

_____

_____

_____

Today's highlights:

_____

_____

_____

_____

Today's challenges:

_____

_____

_____

_____

What are you proud of?

_____

_____

_____

_____

Today's Date: _____

What are you grateful for today?

_____

_____

_____

Today's highlights:

_____

_____

_____

Today's challenges:

_____

_____

_____

What is your greatest strength?

_____

_____

_____

_____

_____

Today's Date: _____

What are you grateful for today?

_____

_____

_____

_____

Today's highlights:

_____

_____

_____

_____

Today's challenges:

_____

_____

_____

_____

What has had the greatest impact on your life and why?

_____

_____

_____

_____

Today's Date: _____

What are you grateful for today?

_____

_____

_____

_____

Today's highlights:

_____

_____

_____

_____

Today's challenges:

_____

_____

_____

_____

What makes you truly happy?

_____

_____

_____

_____

_____

Today's Date: _____

What are you grateful for today?

_____

_____

_____

_____

Today's highlights:

_____

_____

_____

Today's challenges:

_____

_____

_____

What is the hardest part about being a teenager?

_____

_____

_____

_____

_____

Today's Date: _____

What are you grateful for today?

_____

_____

_____

_____

Today's highlights:

_____

_____

_____

_____

Today's challenges:

_____

_____

_____

_____

What are you most afraid of?

_____

_____

_____

_____

Today's Date: _____

What are you grateful for today?

_____

_____

_____

_____

Today's highlights:

_____

_____

_____

Today's challenges:

_____

_____

_____

Do you have any bad habits that you wish you could break? What are they?

_____

_____

_____

_____

_____

Today's Date: _____

What are you grateful for today?

_____

_____

_____

_____

Today's highlights:

_____

_____

_____

Today's challenges:

_____

_____

_____

Do you have any regrets?

_____

_____

_____

_____

_____

Today's Date: _____

What are you grateful for today?

_____

_____

_____

_____

Today's highlights:

_____

_____

_____

_____

Today's challenges:

_____

_____

_____

_____

If you never had to work a day in your life, what would you do?

_____

_____

_____

_____

Today's Date: _____

What are you grateful for today?

_____

_____

_____

_____

Today's highlights:

_____

_____

_____

_____

Today's challenges:

_____

_____

_____

_____

Where do you see yourself in ten years?

_____

_____

_____

_____

_____

Today's Date: _____

What are you grateful for today?

_____

_____

_____

_____

Today's highlights:

_____

_____

_____

_____

Today's challenges:

_____

_____

_____

_____

Do you have a celebrity crush?

_____

_____

_____

_____

_____

Today's Date: _____

What are you grateful for today?

_____

_____

_____

_____

Today's highlights:

_____

_____

_____

Today's challenges:

_____

_____

_____

Is there anything you would like to learn how to do?

_____

_____

_____

_____

Today's Date: _____

What are you grateful for today?

_____

_____

_____

_____

Today's highlights:

_____

_____

_____

_____

Today's challenges:

_____

_____

_____

_____

What are some of your favorite memories?

_____

_____

_____

_____

_____

Today's Date: _____

What are you grateful for today?

_____

_____

_____

Today's highlights:

_____

_____

_____

Today's challenges:

_____

_____

_____

Are you looking forward to being an adult? Why or why not?

_____

_____

_____

_____

_____

Today's Date: _____

What are you grateful for today?

_____

_____

_____

_____

Today's highlights:

_____

_____

_____

Today's challenges:

_____

_____

_____

What is the hardest thing you've ever done?

_____

_____

_____

Today's Date: _____

What are you grateful for today?

_____

_____

_____

_____

Today's highlights:

_____

_____

_____

_____

Today's challenges:

_____

_____

_____

_____

What is the best gift you've ever received?

_____

_____

_____

_____

_____

Today's Date: _____

What are you grateful for today?

_____

_____

_____

_____

Today's highlights:

_____

_____

_____

_____

Today's challenges:

_____

_____

_____

_____

Do you feel good about your friendships?

_____

_____

_____

_____

_____

Today's Date: _____

What are you grateful for today?

_____

_____

_____

_____

Today's highlights:

_____

_____

_____

_____

Today's challenges:

_____

_____

_____

_____

Who is your favorite teacher?

_____

_____

_____

_____

Today's Date: _____

What are you grateful for today?

_____

_____

_____

_____

Today's highlights:

_____

_____

_____

_____

Today's challenges:

_____

_____

_____

_____

What is your favorite and least favorite class?

_____

_____

_____

_____

_____

Today's Date: _____

What are you grateful for today?

_____

_____

_____

_____

Today's highlights:

_____

_____

_____

Today's challenges:

_____

_____

_____

What's the best thing about your parents?

_____

_____

_____

_____

_____

Today's Date: _____

What are you grateful for today?

_____
_____
_____
_____

Today's highlights:

_____
_____
_____
_____

Today's challenges:

_____
_____
_____
_____

If you could go anywhere in the world where would it be
and why?

_____
_____
_____
_____

Today's Date: _____

What are you grateful for today?

_____

_____

_____

_____

Today's highlights:

_____

_____

_____

_____

Today's challenges:

_____

_____

_____

_____

Who is the one person you look up to most? Why?

_____

_____

_____

_____

_____

Today's Date: _____

What are you grateful for today?

_____
_____
_____
_____

Today's highlights:

_____
_____
_____

Today's challenges:

_____
_____
_____

What's your biggest pet peeve?

_____
_____
_____
_____
_____

Today's Date: _____

What are you grateful for today?

_____

_____

_____

_____

Today's highlights:

_____

_____

_____

Today's challenges:

_____

_____

_____

Do you prefer funny or scary movies? Why?

_____

_____

_____

_____

Today's Date: _____

What are you grateful for today?

_____

_____

_____

_____

Today's highlights:

_____

_____

_____

_____

Today's challenges:

_____

_____

_____

_____

Would you rather be the boss or the employee? Why?

_____

_____

_____

_____

_____

Today's Date: _____

What are you grateful for today?

_____

_____

_____

_____

Today's highlights:

_____

_____

_____

Today's challenges:

_____

_____

_____

If you had to eat the same meal every day for the next year, what would you choose?

_____

_____

_____

_____

_____

Today's Date: _____

What are you grateful for today?

_____

_____

_____

_____

Today's highlights:

_____

_____

_____

_____

Today's challenges:

_____

_____

_____

_____

What's the one thing you wish you could tell your younger self?

_____

_____

_____

Today's Date: _____

What are you grateful for today?

_____

_____

_____

_____

Today's highlights:

_____

_____

_____

_____

Today's challenges:

_____

_____

_____

_____

Is it worse to fail miserably at something you want to do, or to never try at all?

_____

_____

_____

_____

_____

Today's Date: _____

What are you grateful for today?

_____

_____

_____

_____

Today's highlights:

_____

_____

_____

Today's challenges:

_____

_____

_____

What is your favorite website?

_____

_____

_____

_____

_____

Today's Date: _____

What are you grateful for today?

_____

_____

_____

_____

Today's highlights:

_____

_____

_____

Today's challenges:

_____

_____

_____

Are you a morning person or a night owl?

_____

_____

_____

_____

Today's Date: _____

What are you grateful for today?

_____

_____

_____

_____

Today's highlights:

_____

_____

_____

_____

Today's challenges:

_____

_____

_____

_____

What is your favorite room in the house and why?

_____

_____

_____

_____

_____

Today's Date: _____

What are you grateful for today?

_____

_____

_____

_____

Today's highlights:

_____

_____

_____

Today's challenges:

_____

_____

_____

What do you want to do after High School?

_____

_____

_____

_____

_____

Today's Date: _____

What are you grateful for today?

_____

_____

_____

_____

Today's highlights:

_____

_____

_____

_____

Today's challenges:

_____

_____

_____

_____

If you could be the best at anything, what would you choose to be good at?

_____

_____

_____

Today's Date: _____

What are you grateful for today?

_____

_____

_____

_____

Today's highlights:

_____

_____

_____

_____

Today's challenges:

_____

_____

_____

_____

Which do you think best describes you – a leader or a follower? Why?

_____

_____

_____

_____

_____

Today's Date: _____

What are you grateful for today?

_____

_____

_____

_____

Today's highlights:

_____

_____

_____

_____

Today's challenges:

_____

_____

_____

_____

Where is your favorite place to be?

_____

_____

_____

_____

_____

Today's Date: _____

What are you grateful for today?

_____

_____

_____

_____

Today's highlights:

_____

_____

_____

Today's challenges:

_____

_____

_____

Would you rather visit the beach or the mountains?

_____

_____

_____

Today's Date: _____

What are you grateful for today?

_____

_____

_____

_____

Today's highlights:

_____

_____

_____

Today's challenges:

_____

_____

_____

What mistake have you made that taught you
something?

_____

_____

_____

_____

_____

Today's Date: _____

What are you grateful for today?

_____

_____

_____

_____

Today's highlights:

_____

_____

_____

Today's challenges:

_____

_____

_____

If you could change your name, what would you change it to?

_____

_____

_____

_____

_____

Today's Date: _____

What are you grateful for today?

_____

_____

_____

_____

Today's highlights:

_____

_____

_____

_____

Today's challenges:

_____

_____

_____

_____

If you had three wishes what would they be?

_____

_____

_____

_____

Today's Date: _____

What are you grateful for today?

_____

_____

_____

_____

Today's highlights:

_____

_____

_____

_____

Today's challenges:

_____

_____

_____

_____

What do you know enough about that you could teach others?

_____

_____

_____

_____

_____

Today's Date: _____

What are you grateful for today?

_____

_____

_____

_____

Today's highlights:

_____

_____

_____

Today's challenges:

_____

_____

_____

What is the greatest thing about being you?

_____

_____

_____

_____

_____

Today's Date: _____

What are you grateful for today?

_____

_____

_____

_____

Today's highlights:

_____

_____

_____

_____

Today's challenges:

_____

_____

_____

_____

What are you struggling with right now?

_____

_____

_____

_____

Today's Date: _____

What are you grateful for today?

_____

_____

_____

_____

Today's highlights:

_____

_____

_____

Today's challenges:

_____

_____

_____

What is your biggest worry?

_____

_____

_____

_____

_____

Today's Date: _____

What are you grateful for today?

_____

_____

_____

_____

Today's highlights:

_____

_____

_____

Today's challenges:

_____

_____

_____

How can you help someone this week?

_____

_____

_____

_____

_____

Today's Date: _____

What are you grateful for today?

_____

_____

_____

_____

Today's highlights:

_____

_____

_____

_____

Today's challenges:

_____

_____

_____

_____

Who do you feel you can talk to about anything?

_____

_____

_____

_____

Today's Date: _____

What are you grateful for today?

_____

_____

_____

_____

Today's highlights:

_____

_____

_____

_____

Today's challenges:

_____

_____

_____

_____

What are you currently working toward?

_____

_____

_____

_____

_____

Today's Date: _____

What are you grateful for today?

_____

_____

_____

_____

Today's highlights:

_____

_____

_____

Today's challenges:

_____

_____

_____

What have you learned about yourself lately?

_____

_____

_____

_____

_____

Today's Date: _____

What are you grateful for today?

_____

_____

_____

_____

Today's highlights:

_____

_____

_____

_____

Today's challenges:

_____

_____

_____

_____

What do you think it takes to be successful?

_____

_____

_____

_____

Today's Date: _____

What are you grateful for today?

_____

_____

_____

_____

Today's highlights:

_____

_____

_____

_____

Today's challenges:

_____

_____

_____

_____

What have you learned about failure?

_____

_____

_____

_____

_____

Today's Date: _____

What are you grateful for today?

_____

_____

_____

_____

Today's highlights:

_____

_____

_____

Today's challenges:

_____

_____

_____

What have you learned about relationships?

_____

_____

_____

_____

_____

_____

Today's Date: _____

What are you grateful for today?

_____

_____

_____

_____

Today's highlights:

_____

_____

_____

_____

Today's challenges:

_____

_____

_____

_____

What's the best part of your family?

_____

_____

_____

_____

Today's Date: _____

What are you grateful for today?

_____

_____

_____

_____

Today's highlights:

_____

_____

_____

_____

Today's challenges:

_____

_____

_____

_____

What is your dream job?

_____

_____

_____

_____

_____

Today's Date: _____

What are you grateful for today?

_____

_____

_____

_____

Today's highlights:

_____

_____

_____

_____

Today's challenges:

_____

_____

_____

_____

What is your favorite food group?

_____

_____

_____

_____

_____

Today's Date: _____

What are you grateful for today?

_____

_____

_____

_____

Today's highlights:

_____

_____

_____

_____

Today's challenges:

_____

_____

_____

_____

How do you make healthy choices?

_____

_____

_____

_____

Today's Date: _____

What are you grateful for today?

_____

_____

_____

_____

Today's highlights:

_____

_____

_____

_____

Today's challenges:

_____

_____

_____

_____

How did you show kindness today?

_____

_____

_____

_____

_____

Today's Date: _____

What are you grateful for today?

_____

_____

_____

_____

Today's highlights:

_____

_____

_____

Today's challenges:

_____

_____

_____

Would you consider yourself an optimist or a pessimist?

_____

_____

_____

_____

_____

Today's Date: _____

What are you grateful for today?

_____

_____

_____

_____

Today's highlights:

_____

_____

_____

_____

Today's challenges:

_____

_____

_____

_____

What gift do you have that you can share with others?

_____

_____

_____

_____

Today's Date: _____

What are you grateful for today?

_____

_____

_____

_____

Today's highlights:

_____

_____

_____

_____

Today's challenges:

_____

_____

_____

_____

Do you love yourself?

_____

_____

_____

_____

_____

Today's Date: _____

What are you grateful for today?

_____

_____

_____

_____

Today's highlights:

_____

_____

_____

_____

Today's challenges:

_____

_____

_____

_____

How do you relax?

_____

_____

_____

_____

_____

Today's Date: _____

What are you grateful for today?

_____

_____

_____

_____

Today's highlights:

_____

_____

_____

Today's challenges:

_____

_____

_____

Do you choose to be happy?

_____

_____

_____

Today's Date: _____

What are you grateful for today?

_____

_____

_____

_____

Today's highlights:

_____

_____

_____

_____

Today's challenges:

_____

_____

_____

_____

How are you a generous person?

_____

_____

_____

_____

_____

Today's Date: _____

What are you grateful for today?

_____

_____

_____

_____

Today's highlights:

_____

_____

_____

_____

Today's challenges:

_____

_____

_____

_____

Do you believe in miracles?

_____

_____

_____

_____

_____

_____

Today's Date: _____

What are you grateful for today?

_____

_____

_____

_____

Today's highlights:

_____

_____

_____

_____

Today's challenges:

_____

_____

_____

_____

What do you think is in outer space?

_____

_____

_____

_____

Today's Date: _____

What are you grateful for today?

_____

_____

_____

_____

Today's highlights:

_____

_____

_____

_____

Today's challenges:

_____

_____

_____

_____

What can you do to help others?

_____

_____

_____

_____

_____

Today's Date: _____

What are you grateful for today?

_____

_____

_____

_____

Today's highlights:

_____

_____

_____

_____

Today's challenges:

_____

_____

_____

_____

What makes you awesome?

_____

_____

_____

_____

_____

Today's Date: _____

What are you grateful for today?

_____

_____

_____

_____

Today's highlights:

_____

_____

_____

Today's challenges:

_____

_____

_____

How can you make a difference in the world?

_____

_____

_____

_____

Today's Date: _____

What are you grateful for today?

_____

_____

_____

_____

Today's highlights:

_____

_____

_____

_____

Today's challenges:

_____

_____

_____

_____

If you could invent something, what would it be?

_____

_____

_____

_____

_____

_____

Today's Date: _____

What are you grateful for today?

_____

_____

_____

_____

Today's highlights:

_____

_____

_____

_____

Today's challenges:

_____

_____

_____

_____

How can you be more positive?

_____

_____

_____

_____

_____

Today's Date: _____

What are you grateful for today?

_____

_____

_____

_____

Today's highlights:

_____

_____

_____

_____

Today's challenges:

_____

_____

_____

_____

What is one thing you would like to change about yourself?

_____

_____

_____

_____

Today's Date: _____

What are you grateful for today?

_____

_____

_____

_____

Today's highlights:

_____

_____

_____

_____

Today's challenges:

_____

_____

_____

_____

What three things have you accomplished this week?

_____

_____

_____

_____

_____

Today's Date: _____

What are you grateful for today?

_____

_____

_____

_____

Today's highlights:

_____

_____

_____

_____

Today's challenges:

_____

_____

_____

_____

What are you looking forward to doing tomorrow?

_____

_____

_____

_____

_____

Today's Date: _____

What are you grateful for today?

_____

_____

_____

_____

Today's highlights:

_____

_____

_____

Today's challenges:

_____

_____

_____

What did you learn today?

_____

_____

_____

_____

Today's Date: _____

What are you grateful for today?

_____
_____
_____
_____

Today's highlights:

_____
_____
_____
_____

Today's challenges:

_____
_____
_____
_____

If you could have one wish, what would it be?

_____
_____
_____
_____
_____

Today's Date: _____

What are you grateful for today?

_____

_____

_____

_____

Today's highlights:

_____

_____

_____

_____

Today's challenges:

_____

_____

_____

_____

How do you have fun?

_____

_____

_____

_____

_____

Today's Date: _____

What are you grateful for today?

_____

_____

_____

_____

Today's highlights:

_____

_____

_____

_____

Today's challenges:

_____

_____

_____

_____

What will you do to step outside your comfort zone this week?

_____

_____

_____

Today's Date: _____

What are you grateful for today?

_____

_____

_____

_____

Today's highlights:

_____

_____

_____

_____

Today's challenges:

_____

_____

_____

_____

What makes you special?

_____

_____

_____

_____

_____

Today's Date: _____

What are you grateful for today?

_____

_____

_____

_____

Today's highlights:

_____

_____

_____

Today's challenges:

_____

_____

_____

Do you like going to school? Why or why not?

_____

_____

_____

_____

_____

_____

Today's Date: _____

What are you grateful for today?

_____

_____

_____

_____

Today's highlights:

_____

_____

_____

Today's challenges:

_____

_____

_____

Do you feel safe?

_____

_____

_____

Today's Date: _____

What are you grateful for today?

_____

_____

_____

_____

Today's highlights:

_____

_____

_____

_____

Today's challenges:

_____

_____

_____

_____

What good deed can you do this week?

_____

_____

_____

_____

_____

Today's Date: _____

What are you grateful for today?

_____

_____

_____

_____

Today's highlights:

_____

_____

_____

_____

Today's challenges:

_____

_____

_____

_____

What's on your heart?

_____

_____

_____

_____

_____

Today's Date: _____

What are you grateful for today?

_____

_____

_____

_____

Today's highlights:

_____

_____

_____

_____

Today's challenges:

_____

_____

_____

_____

What do you dream about?

_____

_____

_____

_____

Today's Date: _____

What are you grateful for today?

_____
_____
_____
_____

Today's highlights:

_____
_____
_____

Today's challenges:

_____
_____
_____

What makes you laugh?

_____
_____
_____
_____
_____

Today's Date: _____

What are you grateful for today?

_____

_____

_____

_____

Today's highlights:

_____

_____

_____

_____

Today's challenges:

_____

_____

_____

_____

What do you do when you're feeling scared?

_____

_____

_____

_____

_____

Today's Date: _____

What are you grateful for today?

_____

_____

_____

_____

Today's highlights:

_____

_____

_____

_____

Today's challenges:

_____

_____

_____

_____

If you could grow up and be famous, what would you
want to be famous for?

_____

_____

_____

_____

Today's Date: _____

What are you grateful for today?

_____

_____

_____

_____

Today's highlights:

_____

_____

_____

_____

Today's challenges:

_____

_____

_____

_____

If you could time-travel, who would you visit and why?

_____

_____

_____

_____

_____

_____

You filled your journal!
Congrats on practicing 90 days of gratitude!

Head to:
www.amazon.com/author/
staceyventimiglia

to order your next journal!

Made in the USA
Coppell, TX
23 April 2021